Strrr-ike!! My First Biography

Emmett Ashford, Baseball Umpire

by

Adrienne Cherie Ashford
(Lewis Bratton)

1663 Liberty Drive, Suite 200
Bloomington, Indiana 47403
(800) 839-8640
www.AuthorHouse.com

© 2004 Adrienne Cherie Ashford (Lewis Bratton)
All Rights Reserved.

No part of this book may be reproduced, stored in a retrieval system, or transmitted by any means without the written permission of the author.

First published by AuthorHouse 10/28/04

ISBN: 1-4184-7762-1 (e)
ISBN: 1-4184-7761-3 (sc)

Library of Congress Control Number: 2004096855

Printed in the United States of America
Bloomington, Indiana

This book is printed on acid-free paper.

Cover illustration: Clarence Stubblefield

Dedication....

This book is dedicated to my niece, Kimberly Hunter, who has been an a ray of sunshine in my life, and the biggest supporter in all of my creative works. She is an elementary school teacher. She is an example of success, outreach, and helping others. She is an excellent example to her students and coworkers. She learned these skills at home and at school.

Kim, live this pride and love. Share it with your students and all others that you meet. It's yours! With love and XXX ……….. Auntie A

Adrienne and Kim, June 2003

Contents...

Dedication....
Introduction
  Chapter 1 A Baby Grows 1
  Chapter 2 Fun in School 13
  Chapter 3 Ready for Work 19
  Chapter 4 Being an Adult 25
  Chapter 5 The Calling 31
  Chapter 6 A Change in Plans 33
  Chapter 7 A Ladder 37
  Chapter 8 The Success 43
  Chapter 9 A New Job 47
  Chapter 10 A Family Reunion 51
The Ending 57
My Dictionary 59
About the Writer 63
Credits 65

Introduction

This is the story of a man who had a dream. He was a man who followed his dream throughout the world of baseball.

The game of baseball began over 15 hundred years ago. Then, people played games with a ball and a stick. After the Civil War, baseball became like the game that we know today.

As time passed, the sport of baseball changed a little. The job of baseball umpire changed a bit , too. But the big change in this job came 100 years later! In the 1960's The Civil Rights Movement in the United States was very strong. It was then that a man named Emmett Ashford became the very first African-American umpire in the major leagues.

    This man was my father. As you read this book, you will see how my father and I are alike. Before I went to kindergarten, I had a book that I scribbled in everyday. My father wrote in his composition book everyday. I loved to write. You will find out that my father loved to write, too. I was the editor of my school newspaper in the 9th grade. I wrote for a famous newspaper called The Los Angeles Sentinel when I was in the 10th grade.

    I did many things in high school. First I had to get good grades. Then I could be in the dance club. I could play tennis. I could learn how to debate, also. You will read about the many things my father did when he was in school.

    I worked a part time job when I was in college just like my Dad. After I became a teacher, I taught teachers how to teach. After my father became an umpire, he taught umpires how to umpire.

A young Emmett Ashford...

My father was a happy and honest man. He loved people. He had bright eyes and a big smile. He always did his best at anything that he tried to do. I am blessed to be like my father. I am blessed because I like to learn. I have learned that I can make my dreams come true just like my father did.

Do not go where the path may lead, go instead where there is no path and leave a trail.

By Ralph Waldo Emerson

Chapter 1
A Baby Grows

My father was Emmett Littleton Ashford. He was born on November 23, 1914 in Los Angeles, California. He was baptized at St. Phillips The Evangelist Episcopal Church in Los Angeles.

Adrienne Cherie Ashford (Lewis Bratton)

His mother was Adele Vain Ragland from Perris, Texas. His father was Littleton Ashford from New York. Littleton was a policeman.

Adele was a writer for a local newspaper. The name of this newspaper was The California Eagle.

Strrr-ike!! - My First Biography

Adele was the office manager of the newspaper. She was the bookkeeper, the billing clerk and ad taker too. She was a very hard worker. This same newspaper was run by Charlotta Bass. Mrs. Bass worked for equal rights for all people. She worked for fairness for people who wanted to buy a house.

Adele didn't make more than $18 each week. So Adele had another job. She worked as the treasurer for her Lodge. Adele was also the daughter of a famous pioneer family in Los Angeles. My grandmother was a fantastic lady!

Adrienne Cherie Ashford (Lewis Bratton)

The house in Los Angeles

My father lived at 721 East 41st Street in Los Angeles. He was happy. In 1916, he got a younger brother. His younger brother was named Wilbur. But things changed. Adele and Littleton were getting a divorce. Now Adele had to pay for the house by herself. She needed time. She had to learn how to take care of two boys by herself. She sent my father to live with Aunt Ettie. Aunt Ettie lived in San Francisco.

Strrr-ike!! - My First Biography

My father was around hard-working people again. Aunt Ettie was a caterer. This was an important job for a Negro then. She was married to Uncle Wiley. Uncle Wiley's family and friends were pioneers in the settlement of northeast Los Angeles in the early 1900s.

My father did very well in San Francisco. He went to Middle School there. He got good grades.

Here are some pages from his composition book.

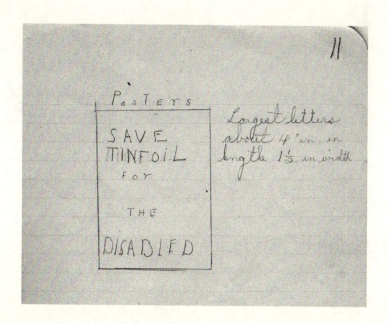

Adrienne Cherie Ashford (Lewis Bratton)

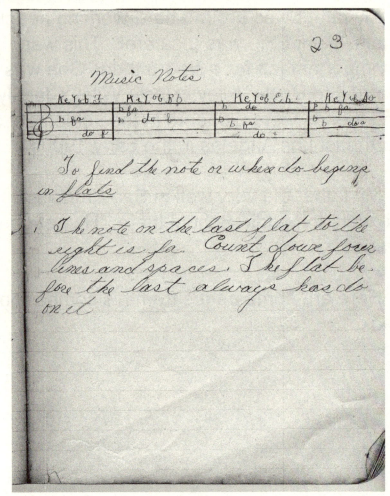

My father liked music.

He was good at writing.

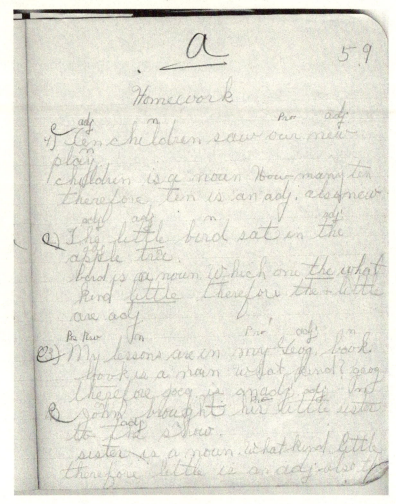

He did his homework.

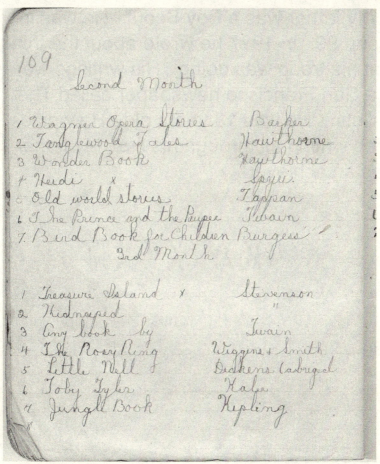

He liked to read, too.

Adrienne Cherie Ashford (Lewis Bratton)

My father was a Boy Scout. He was in Troop 99. In 1927 he wrote about the things that his troop was doing. His writings were in a San Francisco newspaper called The Bulletin. He was 13 years old. He would keep writing all through his life. My father was an achiever!

Strrr-ike!! - My First Biography

My father and Aunt Ettie were very close. Aunt Ettie listened to you. She asked about your feelings. She and Uncle Wiley showed my father many things to learn and many fun activities. I know this is true because I stayed with Aunt Ettie in the summertime. I stayed with Aunt Ettie from the time I was 6 years old until the time I was 11 years old. So I really know about some of the things he did!

I remember.......
riding cable cars,
trips to The Emporium
with Aunt Ettie,
Uncle Wiley's garden,
his talking parrot,
learning to tell time,
running downhill to the
store and coming back
with the right change,
and ooh, the yummy
smell from the
Langendorf bakery when
I woke up.

Chapter 2
Fun in School

When my father came back to Los Angeles he went to Jefferson High School. Many famous people went to Jefferson High School then. My father was in a good place. My father still liked to write. He was a member of the Printers Club. He became co- editor of the school newspaper called the Jeffersonian.

My father wrote outside of school, too. At 16 years old he wrote for the California Eagle newspaper. This was the same newspaper his mother, Adele, worked for. This newspaper was very important to Negroes at that time.

Adrienne Cherie Ashford (Lewis Bratton)

He made up his own column called Ramblin's.

He wrote about Booker T. Washington, too.

Strrr-ike!! - My First Biography

My Dad is in the front row. He is on the left of the teacher.

THOMAS JEFFERSON HIGH SCHOOL 89

JEFFERSONIAN STAFF

Adviser—MISS VIRGINIA CROUCH

Editors-in-Chief	{ Emmett Ashford { Leo Simon
Sport Editor	Joe Cooper
Assistant Sport Editor	Harry Goldberg
Editor Page Two	Emily Jane Greene
Editor Page Three	Rubyline Fillmore
Copy Editor	Bessie Berkowitz
Art	Arthur Katz
Circulation and Mailing Managers	{ Sylvia Koenigsberg { Yoroko Umekubo

REPORTERS

Dolores Erickson	Rio Jow
Thelma Jarvis	Omelia Chatman
Alice Guilford	Phoebe King
Rosalie Dorsey	Joe Marsilisi
Emma Quon	Ilene Harris
Josephine Fierro	Otto Manisto
Leroy Hurt	Cozetta Perry

Adrienne Cherie Ashford (Lewis Bratton)

THOMAS JEFFERSON HIGH SCHOOL 45

TWENTY-EIGHTH STREET HI-Y

President	Leslie Brown
Secretary	Emmett Ashford
Treasurer	John Rout
Athletic Manager	Thomas Collier
Sergeant-at-Arms	James O'Neal

MEMBERS

Ake, George	Childs, Lowell	Mack, Kenneth
Ammons, Milton	Collier, Louis	Minor, Chester
Ammons, Mynyard	Collier, Thomas	O'Neal, James
*Ashford, Emmett	Ferris, Alonso	Pierce, Ovid
Beverly, William	Foster, William	Postell, Joe
Booker, David	Gory, Henton	Roberts, William
Boswell, Posey	Hall, John	Rout, John
*Brewer, John	Harding, Frank	Sapenter, Ernest
Brown, Leslie	Harris, Lewis	Saunders, Julian
Caldwell, Albie	Harris, Morris	Thorne, Kenneth

In 1931, my father was 17 years old. He was the Secretary of the 28th Street Y. This group helped people and worked for the good of the neighborhood. The YMCA still does that today.

Strrr-ike!! - My First Biography

In 1933, my father was president of the Spartans class. He was a senior and he was proud to be doing many things. He was a member of the Scholarship Society because of his good grades. He was a member of the Jefferson Knights. They were ushers during school programs. And he still wrote for the Jeffersonian.

My father did real well in oral language. He helped his classmates in English class. He helped them feel some success. His yearbook said he was famous for scribbling.

My father was a smart dresser. He and his brother, Wilbur, were two of the best dressed guys around the town. My father would always be a great dresser.

My father had great sense of humor, also. He made people laugh and smile. His sense of humor helped him in hard times. This sense of humor made people love him.

Chapter 3
Ready for Work

    As a young man, my father was in a good business and cultural place for Negroes. Central Avenue in Los Angeles was alive! There were businesses and nightclubs. People came to hear the wonderful jazz music. The Dunbar Hotel was important because famous Negroes could stay there. These stars could not stay in the white hotels then.

Dunbar Hotel, 1928
Courtesy
Los Angeles Public Library

Adrienne Cherie Ashford (Lewis Bratton)

My father worked and played in this neighborhood. He was a clerk at Smith's Market. My mother worked across the street. She worked at Woolworth's Five and Dime Store. This is where my father first met my mother, Willa Gene.

When my father and mother were growing up there were no TV's, DVD's, CD's or tapes. So the young people went out alot. My father loved to dance. He was good at it. The Club Alabam was the best place to dance. It was classy too. My father belonged to the Rugcutter's Club. So did my mother. You had to be an excellent dancer to belong to this club. Soon my father and mother became a couple.

My father was still learning. He went to Los Angeles City College. He went to Chapman College. He even learned about Real Estate. He was still an achiever and a smart dresser.

Strrr-ike!! - My First Biography

The Hub of Activity

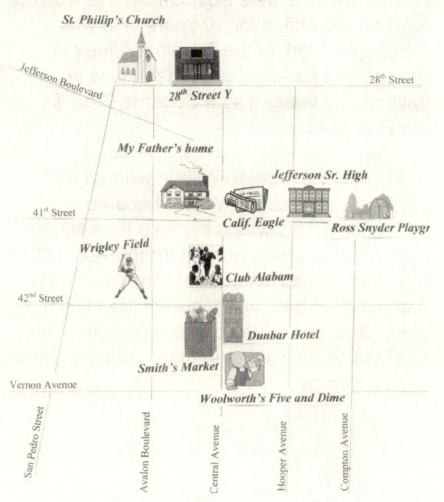

Adrienne Cherie Ashford (Lewis Bratton)

My father took on a new job. He worked for the United States Post Office. He worked for the Post Office for 10 years. He was a Scheme Clerk at the Terminal Annex in downtown Los Angeles. When I was in college .....I worked as a Scheme Clerk for the Post Office too.

My father's brother, Wilbur, worked for the Post Office, also. Wilbur became a supervisor. This was a big step for a Negro then. Wilbur's wife worked for the Post Office too. Her name was Lucille. She became a supervisor like Wilbur. This was really a big step. She was a Negro and a woman. The Post Office gave work to many educated and skilled Negroes then.

Here is my Uncle Wilbur.

Around this time my father thought about how he liked to umpire. The Post Office had baseball teams. These teams played in a league. He worked for the Post Office. So he got to umpire for these games. He was paid only $3.00 an hour. But he loved what he was doing. He did not want to be a baseball player. He wanted to be a baseball umpire!

Chapter 4
Being an Adult

My father really became an adult in 1937. He married my mother, Willa Gene. They were married at St. Phillip's Episcopal Church.

My father and mother surprised everyone when they became engaged. They were very young. They didn't have the wedding until after my mother graduated from Los Angeles High School. She got all A's at Los Angeles High School. My father married smart girl. They were very popular with people their age.

Adrienne Cherie Ashford (Lewis Bratton)

My mother was very pretty. She went to UCLA. Then she became a Playground Director with the City of Los Angeles. She taught the dance classes. She taught ballet and tap dance. She taught Hula dance, too. She taught children and adults.

My father and mother lived on South Van Ness in Los Angeles. Later, they had two girls. One girl was named Antoinette. We called her Toni. The other girl was named Adrienne. That's me !

Adrienne is a baby here.

My family liked to go on trips. We liked to go to the beach. We liked to go see Aunt Ettie in San Francisco. We liked to go to the Easter Egg Hunt in Val Verde, California. I liked the pool there too.

Adrienne and Toni in the backyard on Van Ness

Adrienne Cherie Ashford (Lewis Bratton)

Mama and I at the beach.

Adrienne by the pool in Val Verde. Guess who took the picture.

We liked to go to Murray's Ranch in Perris, California. Noel Lee and Lela Murray owned the ranch. They were my father's kin. Toni and I liked to ride the donkey. Mama helped us get up on the donkey.

Donkey rides.

Strrr-ike!! - My First Biography

My father had to go away for a long time. World War II began. My father was a sailor in the United States Navy. He served from 1944 to 1946. He was trained in three places. He was in Great Lakes, Illinois. He was in Memphis, Tennessee. He learned about Naval Air in Corpus Christi, Texas. He got good grades in the Navy. My father rose to Petty Officer First Class Aircraft Machinery. Wilbur was in the Navy, too. When my father's duty was over, he did not return to the Navy. He wanted to come home. He wanted to be with his family. He wanted to come back to baseball.

Sailors at the National Training Center at Great Lakes in 1943

Photo # 80-G-43078 NTS Great Lakes' Recruit Company 833, August 1943

Adrienne Cherie Ashford (Lewis Bratton)

I was happy when my father was home. I remember a lot of things about my father.

I remember.....

..... going to see my father's kin in Phoenix, Arizona. I saw a teepee in the backyard. I ate honeydew melon for the first time.

.... being careful at the dinner table. My father liked good table manners. You chew your food with your mouth shut. You keep your elbows off the table. You don't sing at the table.

.....my father's neat and trim fingernails.

.....dancing with my father. I learned how to Jitterbug. That dance is called Swing now.

.....getting to see what my father did at work. I saw him umpire. I saw him umpire at a field in Anaheim, California!

Chapter 5
The Calling

After World War II, America began to love baseball. Games were played at night. Now people could see the games after work. The games were aired on the radio. And in 1946, the first baseball game was aired on TV.

It was hard to be an umpire. The fans thought that the umpire was the bad guy. They threw things at the umpire. They called him nasty names. In 1942, the yearly pay for the new umpire was $4,000.00. The umpire had to pay for his food, travel

Chest Protector

and uniforms too. My father still wanted to umpire.

Things began to change. The leagues became bigger. They needed more umpires. The fans liked to see homeruns. Babe Ruth hit a lot of homeruns. This was exciting! An umpire named Bill Klem made people look at the umpire in a new way.

Face Mask

Jackie Robinson was the first Negro to play baseball in a major league. Soon there were others. The wall blocking colored people was coming down.

My father had a dream. He saw the ways that his dream could come true.

Chapter 6
A Change in Plans

Good things were happening to my father in baseball. But his life at home was not so good. My mother wanted him to stay at the Post Office. She wanted him to have a job that he could be sure of.

My mother and father didn't agree on how their money should be spent. My father bought a brand new car. It was a Pontiac.

Adrienne Cherie Ashford (Lewis Bratton)

I remember standing on my tiptoes on the sofa. I stood there everyday. I looked out the window. I waited to see my father come home. I waited to see my father come up the driveway in that car. One day he didn't come up the driveway. He didn't come the next day or the next. Then my grandmother told me to get down off the sofa. She said my father would not come up the driveway again. My mother and father divorced in 1948. It was not a friendly divorce.

Now my father could see us on Sundays. My sister liked to stay at home. Most of the time, my father took me to the ballpark. He took me to Wrigley Field in Los Angeles.

Wrigley Field: photo courtesy of ballparksofbaseball.com

I had my own box seat. The seat was near the base that my father was working on. I could see my father umpire and he could see me. *I remember meeting some of the Angel pitchers before the game. They were warming up. They were tall. I had to look way up!* Sometimes after the games we would visit my father's girlfriend. My mother had married again. I wanted my father to be happy too.

My mother made trips to court for more money to raise Toni and I. Soon there would be no more Sunday visits. The visits to Aunt Ettie would end too. In 1954, my last name was changed from Ashford to Lewis by the court.

My mother's new husband was named Joseph Lewis.

Adrienne Cherie Ashford (Lewis Bratton)

The court's action must have hurt my father deeply. He did something very strange on television. He was on a TV show called This Is Your Life. A famous man called Groucho Marx was the host. Groucho praised him for his work with children. Then Groucho asked him if he had any children of his own. *I held my breath. I was going to hear my name on TV.....but my father told Groucho that he had no children. Oh that hurt!* My father did say he was sorry at a later time.

My father lost other family people around this time. Aunt Ettie died of a heart attack. His brother, Wilbur, died of a heart attack too. Wilbur was young when he died. These events made my father unhappy but he still worked to become an umpire.

Chapter 7
A Ladder

"Kill the umpire!", the fans yelled.

    The fans said bad things to my father because he was an umpire. They said bad things to my father because he was a Negro. My father still wanted to umpire. He still went out to work. He was very brave.

    My father became the first Negro umpire in the pro leagues. He worked in Kansas, Texas and Arizona. He worked games in California too. Then he was made an Umpire in Chief. He was the teacher for other umpires. This was in the 1950s. He was climbing the ladder to his dreams.

Adrienne Cherie Ashford (Lewis Bratton)

My father put fans in the stands. He was still a snappy dresser. He danced around the plate. He made his voice sound like thunder. He was a good showman. He was colorful. Now people could see more games on TV. They liked to see my father.

*Illustration by
Clarence Stubblefield*

A lot of the games were played at Wrigley Field in Los Angeles. My father still had to travel. He went to Oakland, California. Sometimes he even went to Puerto Rico. He liked the music in Puerto Rico. I hear that music today. It is the music people dance Salsa to. Everywhere he went he was happy to sign autographs. The children loved to talk to him.

Photo: Wrigley Field courtesy of
ballparksofbaseball.com

Adrienne Cherie Ashford (Lewis Bratton)

In the middle of the 1950's some people really wanted my Dad to be in the Major Leagues.

Photo: Wrigley Field courtesy of ballparksofbaseball.com

My father had gotten married again. His new wife's name was Margaret. She worked very hard to help my father get that job.

Brad Pye, Jr. worked hard too. He was a writer. He wrote about sports. He wrote about how my father earned the right to be in the big leagues.

My father did excellent work on the field. The big leagues could be another step up the ladder.

Chapter 8
The Success

It was the 1960's. Many things were going to change. Dr. Martin Luther King, Jr. was leading the fight for civil rights. He wanted all people to be treated alike. In 1964, laws were passed for umpires. The laws were for when umpires were on the road. Now all umpires could eat in the same places. Now they could stay in the same hotels as white umpires.

At this time, new umpires had to go to a training school to become an umpire. The job of umpire was lifted to a new level.

Adrienne Cherie Ashford (Lewis Bratton)

In 1966, the American League must have listened to Margaret and Brad Pye, Jr. The American League talked to the Pacific Coast League. The Pacific Coast League let my father go to the American League. My father became the very first Negro or Black major league umpire.

*Illustration by
Clarence Stubblefield*

My father was using skills that he learned while growing up. My father still danced around the plate.

Strrr-ike!! - My First Biography

He twirled and did bunny hops. He was still a neat dresser. His uniform was always pressed. His shoes were always shined. He wore cufflinks and had a handkerchief, too. He still liked to laugh and smile. Laughing helped him to overlook some of the bad things people said about him.

Illustration by Clarence Stubblefield

There were people who thought that a Negro should not be an umpire...and not in the major leagues. My father was always good with people. So he didn't let the bad guys get to him.

Adrienne Cherie Ashford (Lewis Bratton)

    The Television Age was good to my father. The people watching the games could see that my father made good calls. More money came into baseball because of TV. The umpires could work more. When my father wasn't umpiring he took on other jobs. Sometimes he sold beverages. Also, my father had small acting jobs in the 1950's. He was an umpire on an Ironside show called The Terminator. All of this made my father a better showman. He was a wonderful showman for the fans of baseball.

    In 1967 my father was an umpire in the major league All-Star Game. That was another step up the ladder. He got to the top of the ladder in 1970. My father was an umpire in the World Series that year. This was a reward for years of hard work. This was a reward for having faith in himself.

Chapter 9
A New Job

Everyone is the age of their heart.
A proverb from Guatemala

In 1970, my father had to retire. Umpires couldn't work past a certain age. My father wasn't too happy about this.

Things began to look up. Bowie Kuhn, the Commissioner of Baseball, made my father a special assistant. This was a first for a Black man. Then my father was named the Commissioner of the Alaskan Baseball League. This was another first for a Black man.

Adrienne Cherie Ashford (Lewis Bratton)

Photo courtesy of the Los Angeles Sentinel Newspaper

My father had other jobs too. He was the umpire at the Old Timers games at Dodger Stadium in Los Angeles. He umpired for the Celebrity games there too. He umpired at special games at USC. The baseball coach at USC, Ron Dedeaux, made these games happen. I went to one of those games.

I remember.......

seeing Billy Dee Williams, actor, and Lynn Swann, football player and later sportscaster

my father coming out on the field with a cane acting like an old man to be funny

going to an after party at a hall in USC

Tommy Trojan and the horse coming to the party!

My father had more jobs. They were on the screen. In 1976, he played the plate umpire in the movie, Bingo Long and His Travelling All Stars. He was yelling, "Play ball"! Around that time he was a weekly guest on the TV show, The Jacksons. He played different parts. He liked working with the famous Jackson Five kids.

Adrienne Cherie Ashford (Lewis Bratton)

In 1977 my father went to Nevada. A lot of celebrities went there too. They went to the 11th Annual World Chili Cookoff. This Cookoff was held every year. It was a contest. People came and cooked their own best chili. My father was the umpire and scorekeeper for the big cookoff. That was hot stuff!

What a link to my Dad! I cook 3 kinds of chili every December. I think my guests would say that I am a chili-making winner.

It was becoming fun to be retired.

Chapter 10
A Family Reunion

Your father is a humble man.
Margaret Ashford

Retirement had more surprises for my father. It all began with my husband, Jimmy. He knew that I missed seeing my father. He said there was a number in the telephone book. He said that I should call that number. I did.

Margaret answered the phone. She wanted to meet me for lunch before I could talk to my father. She did not know that he had any children. My father's co-workers didn't know that he had children. When I first

Adrienne Cherie Ashford (Lewis Bratton)

saw her, I thought about how much she looked like my mother. She looked at me a for long time. Then she said, "You are your father's child". She talked to my father when she went home. My father called me.

Cassius

My father and Margaret invited me to their house for lunch. Margaret loved to cook. She had a very modern kitchen. She loved to have people come over. I met their dog, Strike. *Strike looked just like my dog, Cassius!* The first time that my father and I were alone, he told me how sorry he was about what he said to Groucho Marx. My father must have had that on his mind all of these years.

Soon Jimmy and I had them over for dinner. My father loved our dog, Cassius. All four of us went out to dinner too.

Strrr-ike!! - My First Biography

My father and I got to know each other again. He liked what I had become since he last saw me. He was proud that I was a teacher. He thought it was a wonder that I learned Hindu dance and Belly Dance. He gave me the nickname "Stuff".

I was glad that my father asked me what I thought about baseball. My thoughts helped him with his job as Special Assistant to the Commissioner, Bowie Kuhn.

Daddy and me

In many ways, I think my father was trying to make up for not being in my life for a long time. He liked my ideas. He sent me his cleaning lady, Sonia. He called me about the TV mini series, Roots. When he called, he said he was "Kunte Kinte". Kunte Kinte was the leading part. It was played by LeVar Burton.

Adrienne Cherie Ashford (Lewis Bratton)

Sometimes we danced. We danced Samba. Samba is the dance of Brazil. My father liked Brazil. My father was still the father I loved when I was a little girl. He was fun and playful.

My father was very happy until 1978. This was the year that his beloved Margaret passed away. Margaret was sick but she didn't tell my father. He became very lonely. My father didn't want to call me because he didn't want to make me sad. I began to worry about my father. Sonia began to worry, too. She said everything in his house was the same as it was when Margaret was alive. Nothing was ever moved. My father said that I was all that he had.

Daddy and Margaret

*Illustration by
Clarence Stubblefield*

In time my father was ready to date. He moved to Marina Del Rey, California. He didn't have to climb stairs there. This was better for his heart. Sonia cleaned there too. One day she told me that she had picked up glasses for **two.** Later he remarried.

My father was there for me when my marriage ended. He said things that were very helpful. He wanted me to date. He fixed up one or two dates for me. He didn't pick the baseball players. He picked sportscasters.

Daddy and I

Adrienne Cherie Ashford (Lewis Bratton)

On March 1, 1980, something very sad happened in my life. My father, Emmett Ashford, died of a heart attack. He died just like Aunt Ettie and his brother, Wilbur. I am so glad that I got to know him after I grew up.

To remember him, a Little League Ballpark on the Westside of Los Angeles was named for him. The Emmett Ashford Community Spirit Award began. To win this award you have to do excellent work and help others. This award is a wonderful example of my father's spirit.

The Ending

The game of baseball changed a lot from 1950 to 2000. The umpires got a union. The starting pay was now $11,000. Now umpires were judges - not bad guys. More people bought TVs. More people saw the games on TV. More people saw my father, Emmett Ashford. And more people loved him.

My father was a Sagittarius. This is a zodiac sign. The colors for this sign are navy blue and maroon. Umpire uniforms are these colors. My father was in a uniform that was just right for him!

Emmett Ashford

My Dictionary

A
achiever - a person who makes things happen; a person who carries out a plan
apprentice - a person who is learning a craft or trade
autograph - name written by a famous person who wrote it himself or herself

B
beverages - drinks

C
caterer - one who provides food and waiters for parties
civil rights - rights that belong to the people
classy - first class, elegant, in style
college - school after Grade 12, university
commissioner - a person who runs and makes rules for a pro sport
couple - two people
credential - a paper that shows one's right to a job

cultural - about the arts and skills of a group of people

D
dancesport - ballroom dance showings
daughter - a girl child
debate - to talk about the reasons for or against something
dedicated - giving, devoted
degree - credit for finishing the classes at a college

E
editor - one who edits writings for a newspaper or magazine; one who writes for a newspaper or magazine using her own ideas
educated - one who has learned a lot; finished school or college
engaged - planning to get married

G
graduated - finished all work at a school or college

H
honest - truthful
humble - simple, not phony
humor - fun, makes one laugh

J
journal - a daily record of one's life

K
kin - family

L
league - group of sports teams
legacy - anything handed down from ancestors
lodge - the hall or building of a club

M
major - bigger, more important

minor - smaller in size, less important
multi - many

N
naval - about the navy
Negro - the name given to the offspring of the slaves that came to the United States from Africa

P
pioneer - one who is the first to do something

R
real estate - land, property

S
scribble - write messy
settlement - colony, new place to live
snappy - neat, lively
supervisor - person who oversees the work of others

T
teepee - a cone shaped tent that Native Americans lived in

treasurer - one who takes care of the money for a group

U
umpire - judge, referee
uniform - suit used in a job
union - a group that helps working people
urban - in the city

About the Writer

Photo: Michael Hiller

Adrienne Cherie Ashford, daughter of Emmett Ashford and Willa Gene Fort, attended UCLA where she got a degree and Teaching Credential. Later, she attended Cal State University at Los Angeles where she got her Master's degree in Urban Education.

She was a classroom teacher, a training teacher and a Teacher Advisor for the Los Angeles Unified School District.

Adrienne does many other things too. She is an actor. She has been in ads, on film and TV. She's a dancer and dance teacher. She's a cowriter and dancer in a program to bring fine arts to children. This program is called Welcome to the Multicultural World of Dancesport. Lastly, she's the editor of a dance magazine.

Credits

Acknowledgements and Appreciations...

Allison, John – Senior High classmate, commentary

Ashford, Lucille – Sister in Law, my Aunt, inspiration

Bailey, Mrs. - Head Librarian, Jefferson Senior High School

Cross, Gene – Fan: Actor, Writer, Photographer, childhood memories

Hunter, Kimberly – My Niece…sunshine, eternal supporter, critic

Landill, Mark – Video Archivist, Dodger Stadium

Lewis, Willa Gene – 1st Wife, my Mom with memories

Lomax, Almena - colleague of Adele Ashford, former writer for The California Eagle

Mackie, Myrna – 1st Cousin, lived with Aunt Ettie, photos, wordbook and news articles

Perez, Reverend Altagarcia – Pastor St. Phillips Episcopal Church, records

Smith, Helen Broyles – Father's contemporary, news articles

Van Cleave, Kendra – Researcher, USC, isd archives, resources

Books

Brooks, Tim and Marsh, Earle. <u>Complete Directory of Primetime Network and Cable Shows: 1946 – present.</u> New York, Ballantine Books, 1995

Rust, Art Jr. <u>Get That Nigger Off The Field.</u> Brooklyn, NY: Book Mail Services, 1992, p. 78

Magazine and Newspaper Articles

Ashford, Emmett. "Booker T. Washington's Life Story" <u>California Eagle</u> 4 April 1930: p.8

Ashford, Emmett. "Boy Scout Page of the Bulletin: Troop 99" <u>San Francisco Home Newspaper</u> 4 May 1927: C10

Ashford, Emmett, "Ramblins of the Young Folks", <u>California Eagle</u> 20 February 1931 pp 9-12

Jackson, Steve. "Ashford: A Patient Pioneer Passes Quietly" <u>Los Angeles Times</u> 7 March 1980: *PP*

Pye, Brad Jr. "Big Umpire in the Sky Calls Emmett Ashford Out" Los Angeles Sentinel 6 March 1980

Robinson, Jesse L. " That's Sports: Emmett Ashford – One of the Best" The Compton Bulletin 12 March 1980: Section 2 , 6

Shalit, Gene. "Ultra Ump" Look Magazine", 4 October 1966 (Vol. 30, Issue 25), p.92 (5 pages)

Staff. "Ashford Arrives: Flamboyant Ump Finally Makes Big Time", Ebony Magazine, June, 1966 (Vol. 21, Issue 8), p.65 (5 pages)

Staff. "Los Angeles Post Office: Pattern of Democracy" Pittsburgh Courier 4 February 1950: II 1

Staffwriter. "Announce Engagement of Willa Gene Fort and Emmett Ashford" The California Eagle 31 December 1936:

Young, A. S. (Doc). "Ashford Gave Up Safe Job to Become History Maker" <u>Los Angeles Sentinel</u> 6 March 1980:

Website or Webpage

Gerlach, Larry R. <u>Umpires.</u> 8/18/98 <http://www.totalbaseball.com>

Heitz, Thomas R. <u>Encarta</u>. 8/18/98 <http;//www.totalbaseball.com/history/people/umpire>

http://www.ballparksofbaseball.com/past/lawrig

http://www. history.navy.mil/photos/images

http://home.att.net/~quotationsexchange

http://www.home.pcmagic.net/torpedo/Wade472807   (vintage cars)

http://www.imdb.com (international movie database)

http://www.pbs.org/blackpress/news_bios/bass.html

http://www.quotationspage.com

http://www.stanford.edu/group/King

http://www.usc.edu/dunbar/IMAGES
(Wrigley Field)

http://www.usc.edu/isd/locations/ssh/doheny/ref/BHM/biddy_mason.html

Additional Resources

A.C. Bilbrew Library, California Eagle, Microfiche Reel #11

Los Angeles Central Library, History: California Eagle, Microfilm 1936-1937, 1930 -1931

United States Naval Personnel, Records

Made in the USA
Las Vegas, NV
12 March 2024

87083868R00052